THE BIG BOOK OF FARTS

BY
JAMES CARLISLE

For Aiden, Archie, Elias, Julius and Samuel

Published by the Sovereign Media Group.

INDEX

Introduction..7

Funny Fart Facts: 9

What Type of Fart Was That? 19

    The Great Pretenders...19

    The Real Deal:..21

    Party Farts...22

    Animal Farts:...23

The Great Farts of History 29

    The Fart That Deposed A King..29

    The Roman Fart That Killed Thousands...................................30

    The Fart that Cast a Vote...31

    The World Famous French Fart-Man 33

    Adolf Hitler's Deadly Farts 35

Fart Jokes...37

Farty one liners 45

Fart Poems and Limericks 47

Farting Romeos...50

Why we fart...51

Fart Fixes...57

Bottom Blast Etiquette, To Fart or not to fart?................................61

    The Elevator:...61

    The Dinner Table: 62

    The Job Interview: 62

    The Big Date:...63

    Farting in an Airplane...63

Farting around the world 65

Fart Shame..66

Farting At The Movies...67

Arty Farty – The Farts in High Art 73

Great Farts of Literature 77

    Shakespeare. 77

    Dante Alighieri 81

    Geoffrey Chaucer 81

    Ben Johnson 82

    Mark Twain 82

    Aristophanese 84

    James Joyce 84

    1001 Arabian Night's Tales. 84

    John Aubrey 85

    J.D. Salinger 85

    Francois Rabelais. 86

    Benjamin Franklin - The Founding Farter. 88

A fart By Any Other Name. 93

Fart Onomatopoeia. 99

A Farty Farewell. 101

Introduction

Much as some of us hate to admit it, everybody LOVES a good fart. Move over belches, coughs, sneezes, vomits, snot and boogers, forget number ones and number twos, farts are the undisputed superstars of bodily functions.

It is an inalienable truth; a fart is always funny!

Farts have been a constant source of entertainment and pleasure throughout human history. From Arisotle to Shakespeare, from Benjamin Franklin to Mark Twain, some of the greatest minds that have ever lived have loved a good fart gag.

No one is ever really upset or angry at a fart. Even if it smells horrible, a good fart will still make us smile. After all, nothing can diffuse a tense situation and have everyone falling about with laughter faster than a well-placed F bomb. Let's face it, there is nothing that livens up a boring party like a deafeningly loud rectal honk.

Everyone has their own idea of exactly what constitutes a perfect fart. For me a perfect fart takes time to ferment. It must have a good fruity bouquet, and a loud robust tone. It should be reasonably dry (not wet and sloppy), and bring a smile to the face of anyone in close proximity.

If it fails to get a laugh it was either too quiet, or just not stinky enough (or both).

Butt no matter what kind of backside blasters you love I am delighted that you have chosen to take this journey into the wonderful world of farts with me. There is so much to know and celebrate about the humble bottom belch, and by the end of this book you should be an expert. So sit back and relax and prepare yourself to learn all about the humble backfire.

Funny Fart Facts

What better way to launch into the endlessly fascinating subject of flatulence than with a few prize fart facts? Armed with such an enthralling array of knowledge about all things related to butt gas you are bound to be the life of any party! So lets get started….

Taming your stinky fart pants: Did you know you can actually get underwear with a charcoal lining to neutralize the stench of a good fart? Sold as "odor-proof undies", "shreddies" or "under-ease" these specially made undies are designed to filter out the stink before your fart escapes your pants… AMAZING!!

Mmmm Fish Farts Yummy I smell dinner

Farting Fish: Did you know that both herring and salmon communicate through farting? It's true! According to a study conducted by a Canadian university both herring and salmon emit fast, repetitive ticks from their butts to communicate with each other. Apparently they blow off a few bubbles to warn each other about nearby whales. Trouble is the whales can hear their little bum blurts and they home in for a frenzied feast of farting fish. Mother nature can be so cruel!

All the Farts in History: It has been estimated that if you added up all the bottom blasts by all the humans that have ever lived, it would add up to approximately 17 quadrillion farts. (That's 17,000,000,000,000,000 farts)

Fart jokes date back at least 5000 years: According to professor Paul McDonald of the University of Wolverhampton the world's oldest fart joke dates back to 1900 BC in ancient Sumerian times. The joke was a one-liner, and really not all that funny: *"Something that has never occurred since time immemorial? A young woman did not fart in her husband's lap".*

Hitler was relentless farter: Apparently the insane 20th century dictator Adolf Hitler was plagued by gastric problems that caused him to blow the ass bugle almost non-stop. He was said to have taken 28 different medications to try and fix his raging trouser cough but to no avail. Of course being a violently insane dictator no one was prepared to call him stinky pants; or at least not to his face.

You can get a pill to make your farts smell like roses: An elderly French inventor was so sick of choking on other peoples fetid backside stench that he invented a pill that makes farts

smell like roses, (you can also get them in chocolate smell!). The pills which are made of all natural ingredients such as seaweed, blueberries and fennel, have been approved by health authorities. They are also available for dogs, (yes we believe you, you are buying them for for the dog!).

Air travel makes you fart: Yes, there's more than one reason they call frequent fliers "the jet set". Scientifically speaking the difference in air pressure between your gut and the passenger cabin makes building up a reservoir of noxious ass gas practically inevitable. Naturally all that gas has to escape to somewhere and the only place it can go is into the passenger cabin. This is rather unfortunate when you consider that the cabin air is recycled. When you are up in the air your farts can quite literally hang around like a bad smell for hours afterwards!

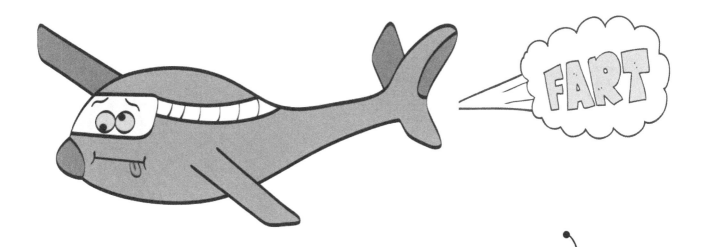

Some beetles fart to attract a mate: The female Southern Pine Beetle lets off a spectacular rectal honk in order to attract males. This beetle pops off a pheromone-laden love puff so pungent that all the boys come running.

You can't fart at the bottom of the ocean: When scuba divers get down more than 33 feet below sea level the water pressure is so great that their digestive gases can no longer form bubbles, which leaves their food just festering inside their colons. Yuck!!

Fart sniffing can actually be good for you: Those canny researchers at Exeter University have discovered that sniffing small quantities of hydrogen sulfide (the stink gas in farts) can help prevent heart attacks, stroke, cancer and dementia, as well as helping to reverse small amounts of genetic damage... so breath deep my lovelies!

Don't say "hi", just let one rip: Cultural habits vary all over the world. What might seem gross to us is perfectly acceptable to others. For example the South American Yanomami tribe find the best way to greet someone is to peel off a quick friendly blast of anal thunder. Could this curious custom be the origin of the parting quip *"smell you later"*?

Dead bodies can go on farting for hours after death: Did you know that the human body can keep on pumping out air tulips for up to four hours after death? In fact your butt can keep on singing right up until rigor mortis sets in.

Fart sniffing is a lucrative career in some places: In China there are some savvy folk that make good money sniffing people's poop gophers. There are those that can accurately diagnose digestive illnesses by the piquant aromas of someone's air biscuits and are paid quite handsomely for their remarkable skill.

Want to know many farts in an H-bomb? You have to love science. All those dedicated nerds out there working hard to find out all the really

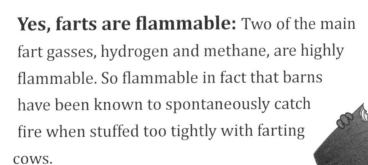

important stuff. Well here it is, it would take one person almost 80 million years of continual farting to generate enough energy for one small atomic bomb. However if we all got together on this and everyone on the planet ripped the equivalent of 66.6 million farts simultaneously we would produce enough energy to make a single H-Bomb.

Yes, farts are flammable: Two of the main fart gasses, hydrogen and methane, are highly flammable. So flammable in fact that barns have been known to spontaneously catch fire when stuffed too tightly with farting cows.

Termites are the world champion farters: According to the EPA those pesky little wood-munchers produce a staggering 11% of the world's methane emissions.

"Global emissions of methane due to termites are estimated to be between 2 and 22Tg per year, making them the second largest natural source of methane emissions. Methane is produced in termites as part of their normal digestive process, and the amount generated varies among different species." - EPA

In order to protect their nests some "soldier" termites have the ability to blow themselves up, spraying their attackers with a noxious blend of termite fart and faeces in a process called "autothysis." What's more, fossilized termite farts have even discovered trapped in amber.

Toys that make fart noises have been around for centuries: It is a testament to the enduring popularity of farts that devices for simulating fart noises go back at least as far as Roman times.

The trend took on global pop-ularity in 1920 with the invention of the whoopi cushion, *(they didn't call them the roaring 20's for nothing),* but has reached giddy new heights with the advent of 21st century fart noise apps.

There are now literally thousands of fart noises available for download as ring tones, or just to play at your leisure. Wet ones, long ones, short ones; you can get a special fart noise for every occasion imaginable.

Farts like the nightlife: Just like vampires, most farts only come out at night. You will do approximately 70-80% of your daily farts while you are tucked up in bed at night.

Spot the difference: It is the nerve endings in your colon and sphincter that distinguish the difference between a fart and a poop, but sometimes they can get confused. When your poop is more runny than usual they can get it tragically wrong and leave you with an embarrassing mud butt! (Lucky for all of us this doesn't happen very often, or it would be… well… totally gross).

Girl's farts smell worse: Sorry ladies it's true. Science has looked into it and discovered that when men and women eat the same food women produce a more concentrated, and thus more stinkarific gas than men.

Maggot farts have antibiotic properties: I am not sure how exactly they figured this out but maggot farts can help stave off bacterial infections. Scientists are working hard to turn maggot farts into medicine.

Some creatures can never fart: Jellyfish, sea anemones and corals can never ever fart because they do not have an anus.

The USA has a National Pass Gas Day: Yes people it's true, following hot on the heels of National Bean Day is January 7th, National Pass Gas Day. Just makes you want to cheer ...USA... USA... USA!!!!

Also makes you wonder why the greeting card industry hasn't got on to this? A scratch and sniff card would be just the thing for such a hallowed occasion.

Less than 1% of a fart smells: It's true, less than 1% of the average fart contains chemicals that actually stink. However our noses know how to pick up the stinky wafts in minute concentrations. In fact humans can smell the stinky part of a fart at levels as low as 1 part in 100 million.

The recipe for an average fart: There are many different types of farts, but in a typical fart you might expect to find the following mix: 1% hydrogen sulphide (the smelly part), 7% methane, 21% hydrogen, 59% nitrogen, 9% carbon dioxide and 4% oxygen.

The longest fart: The worlds longest recorded fart was pumped out by one Bernard Clemmens of London, who according to the Guinness Book of Records managed to let off a butt blast with the utterly staggering duration of 2 minutes, 42 seconds.

The speed of Farts: Farts have been clocked travelling at speeds of 10 feet per second, which is about 7mph.

Law breaking boomers: For some rather inexplicable reason it is apparently illegal to fart in a public place in Florida, after 6pm on a Thursday, due to some ludicrous long forgotten law that is surprisingly still on the books.

Toilet time: Not quite a fart fact, but interesting none the less. Did you know that the average person spends three years of their life on the toilet?

What Type of Fart Was That?

There are hundreds of different types of farts, and it would be almost impossible to list them all. However there are some perennial favorites that we all know and love.

In this section we will look at the most common types of everyday farts. How long would it take you to spot one of every kind of fart on the list?

The Great Pretenders

The great pretenders are just that; pretend farts! Mostly they are considered fake because they come from some body part other that the butt; but while many pretenders make a thunderously raucous noise they usually don't smell at all.

The Raspberry:

This perennial favorite is made by blowing air through closed lips with the tongue poked out a little. In the more advanced, and far more intricate raspberry ripple one blows under the tongue at the start giving you the low note and over the tongue at the end for the classic finish on the high note.

Often performed by grandparents on baby's bellies, the raspberry is not considered either rude or particularly funny... unless of course you are baby, in which case it is totally hilarious!

The Armpit fart:

The armpit fart has long been popular as a party starter, or a tension breaker, (particularly in high pressure situations like siting down to do an exam).

While I have seen APF's done by others, try as I might (and believe me I have tried), I have not been able to pump one of these beauties out myself, so unfortunately I cannot give you any advice on how it is done.

The Brain Fart:

Just like real farts everyone drops a brain fart now and again. A brain fart is simply a stupid idea or comment that slips through your filter and gets said out loud.

Of course being both silent and odorless they don't always get called out immediately, but in most cases anyone with half a brain can spot one pretty well instantly.

The Emoji Fart:

They say a picture paints a thousand words; well thanks to modern technology and some whacky graphic artists, you can now send someone a butt puff even when you are lost for words.

The Real Deal

The SBD:

The silent but deadly is the most feared of all farts, the SBD creeps up like a stealthy ninja warrior and kapoweee!!!, You get blasted with the billowing cloud of putrid ass stinkery. Due to its sneaky silence the culprit is rarely if ever caught.

The Side Squeezer:

This little popper is most often used when one is seated for long periods of time, like in an airplane, or some other stressful situation. The dealer gently lifts one butt cheek up off their chair and quietly opens the gas tank.

Most side squeezers are silent, but easily spotted by the dealer's leaning sideways. Unless it is mind bogglingly malodorous its best not call anyone out on a side squeezer, as they are usually trying to let out a quick poot under the radar.

The Rump Ripper:

The rump ripper is totally out there, loud and proud. It is that powerful backside roar that announces its own arrival louder than a Kardashian! The rump ripper often has a full bodied, fruity aroma, and just like a proud parent its dealer is usually delighted to take full credit.

The Bubble Bath:

The bubble bath is proof that anyone with a bathtub and an overactive cheek slapper can enjoy a relaxing spa. Of course it is much more fun when there is someone else in the bath with you!

The Party Fart

Pull my finger:

An oldie butt a goodie, pull my finger goes down especially well with toddlers. When you are about to fart you simply invite someone to pull your finger. As they pull, you push, and if all goes according to plan you should fart at exactly the right moment. I promise you this is gut bustlingly funny for anyone under 6.

The Whoopi cushion:

The whoopi cushion, that little rubber bladder of farty fun that gets hidden under the throw rug, has been around for about 100 years, and has remained steadfastly popular the whole time.

A whoopi cushion is just the thing to loosen up an uptight teacher, boss, parent or sibling. In fact anyone who takes themselves too seriously and needs to get over themselves is fair game when it comes to the whoopi cushion.

Flamethrowers and bottom rockets:

Even though many dim dudes have thought that lighting their own flamethrower would impress their friends and win them the girl of their dreams, everyone knows that only a TOTAL IDIOT would want to set his own wind tunnel on fire.

You are far more likely to end up torching your house and being admitted to the burns unit of your local hospital than winning the admiration of your friends (or that cute girl from down the street).

Animal Farts:

The world is literally teeming with top 10 lists, but here is one you won't come across every day. The top 10 farting animals:

1. Termites: Not only can these pesky little insects chomp your house into oblivion, they will fart up a storm while they are at it! These little wood munchers are by far the biggest producers of methane on the planet, producing a whopping 11% of the world's methane emissions all on their own. Holy Farts!

2. Camel Farts: Camels may be champion farters, but strangely enough camel's farts are not the worst smell to come from these ships of the desert. I have it on good authority that it camel stench is equally vile whether you stand in front of, or behind a camel. By all accounts camels breath is so unspeakably evil it could curl your toes.

Here's an interesting factoid: A few years back the Australian government decided that the methane in camel farts was destroying the environment. Supposedly all that rancid camel butt gas was pushing up Australia's greenhouse gas emissions; so they decided to shoot all the feral camels. Fortunately for the Camels the plan was pretty well laughed out of parliament, so they got to live to fart another day... Hooray!!

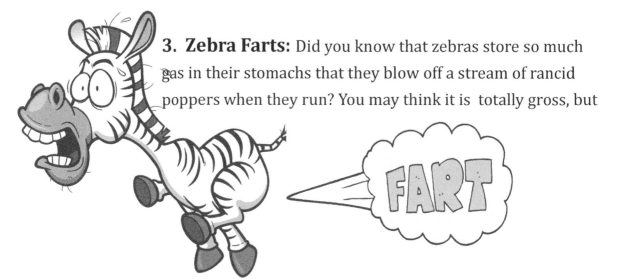

3. Zebra Farts: Did you know that zebras store so much gas in their stomachs that they blow off a stream of rancid poppers when they run? You may think it is totally gross, but maybe all that stink is part of their cunning plan to keep those hungry lions at a bay; after all a stink bomb like that going off in your face would be enough to put anyone off their food.

4. Sheep Farts: Sheep may be only fourth on the list of most farty animals, but that doesn't stop their pumps from causing total mayhem. Apparently in 2015 a Boeing 747 was forced to make an emergency landing when the farts from the 2,186 sheep it was carrying built up so much methane in the fuselage that the smoke alarms went off.

But seriously, there are over a billion sheep in the world and that adds up to one massive motherlode of methane. So much in fact that scientists in New Zealand are working on vaccine to neutralize the microbes that make sheep farts. Imagine being able to get vaccinated against farts, how amazing is that?

5. Cow Farts: According to the EPA, cows are among the top methane makers. The rumen (pre stomach) of a cow can hold between 40 to 60 gallons of material with approximately 150 billion microorganisms per teaspoon. With such a fermenting cauldron bubbling away inside them it's no surprise that cows are blasting their butts off almost nonstop, releasing between 550 and 1,100 pounds of methane per day.

According to the Journal of Experimental Biology, nearly 30 percent of the Earth's methane emissions originate from animal farts.

6. Elephant Farts: Don't ever stand directly behind an elephant. Not only is an elephants butt hole at about the same height as most people's faces, the sound can be so loud you could end up going deaf in one ear. In fact when it comes to billowing backside thunder all pachyderms (be they elephant, hippo or rhino) can really pack a good gaseous wallop!

7. Dog Farts: Dogs may be man's best friends but dog farts remain among the most rancid and foul smelling things ever to enter a human nostril. In fact the rectal stench of K9 back blasters have been plaguing human populations for tens of thousands of years.

There a lot of different reasons we put up with our Fido's stinky dog butt, but the main reason is so we can have someone to blame our own stinkoid bottom cheek claps on. Best of all, as Fido can't speak he can't deny it!

8. Vegetarian Humans: Ok, while not eating meat may be great for the animals, and help reduce your carbon footprint, it will turn you into a human rectal stink burger. There can be no question; all those soybeans come at a cost to your domestic air quality. As anyone who has ever had a macrobiotic hippie come to stay, vegetarians are champions when it comes to opening the basement window.

9. Non Vegetarian Humans: Ok, well maybe it is not just the vegetarians. Meat eating humans can pretty ripe in the trouser department too. In fact there really isn't all that much in it, so if you are planning to chow down on a cow to keep your rump mist under control then you might be disappointed.

10. Gerbils: The poor old gerbil is the butt of many a joke, but maybe there is good reason. These cute little munchkins can blow the backside horn like there is no tomorrow, which is of course why they have earned their place on the farting top ten.

Contrary to what some people think gerbils are not hamsters. Not only do gerbils pump from the rump with far more gusto than their hamster cousins, they have long furry tails with a little puff of fur at the end.

11. Cat Farts: While cats miss out on the top 10, they are one of the animals whose farts we humans get to savor the most. But did you know you will almost never hear a cat fart? In fact cats are notorious for their SBDs.

Being true masters of the silent pop tart, cats will sneak up on you like a ninja, drop some foul fanny fog and make a stealthy getaway before you even knew they were there. Of course we forgive them because they are so cute and fluffy.

28

The Great Farts of History

The Fart That Deposed A King

According to that rockin' Greek historian Herodotus, one little fart lead to an all out rebellion against King Apries of Egypt, who was, (by all accounts) a bit of an ass and had absolutely no sense of humor.

It started In 569 B.C. when Apries sent one of his generals, Amasis, to put an end to a rebellion among some of his troops. Instead of bringing the disgruntled soldiers back into line the troops declared Amasis to be their new king.

Needless to say Apries was not happy with this turn of events, so he sent one of his advisors, a popular dude named Patarbemis to persuade the unruly mob to submit to his rule. According to Herodotus, Amasis let rip with a deafening blast and told Patarbemis to "take that back to Apries." Being a dutiful emissary Patarbemis sent forth a messenger immediately to deliver Amasis's reply.

Somewhat unsurprisingly Apries was not best pleased and proceeded to have the messenger's nose and ears cut off.

Unfortunately for Apries news of his brutally torturing the poor messenger swept though the land and turned the whole of Egypt against him. In spite of having been their king Apries ended up being torn apart by a rabid mob. Amasis on the other hand ended up ruling from 569 to 525 B.C. The moral of this story is obvious; farts are funny, so don't take offence!

The Roman Fart That Killed Thousands.

As totally unbelievable as it sounds in 44 A.D in Jerusalem a fart actually led to the deaths of thousands of people. The exact number of fatalities are unknown, but estimates range from five thousand to thirty thousand depending on who you believe.

In the 75 A.D. bestseller, The Jewish War the famous historian Flavius Josephus, (37-100) describes an incident in which a rather rude anti-Semitic Roman soldier uncovered his backside for a crowd of Jews celebrating Passover. In the words of Josephus the rather ill advised centurion "pulled back his garment, and cowering down after an indecent manner, turned his breech to the Jews, and spake such words as you might expect upon such a posture."

Naturally such a blatant act of disrespect on such a holy occasion got some of the Jews hoping mad and they began stoning the soldiers. Horrified by the attack on his troops the Roman governor of Jerusalem, Cumanus (no joke), called in the riot squad at which point it was ON!

Unfortunately for the Jews most of them were crowded into the temple grounds when the Roman army arrived, which gave the Roman soldiers a serious strategic advantage. While a few Roman soldiers were killed most of the dead were Jews killed in the human stampede trying to escape the Temple.

As far as anyone knows this is the greatest single loss of life ever directly attributed to a fart.

The fart that cast a vote in the British parliament

In 1607, British Member of Parliament Henry Ludlow was sitting in the house of commons during a debate about naturalizing the Scots when he let off an ass honker so loud that it was counted as dissenting vote. The farting nay-vote was no doubt an accident, but it passed into folklore inspiring one of the most famous fart poems in history:

The Censure of the Parliamentary Fart.

*Never was bestowed such art
upon the tuning of a Fart.*

*Down came grave auntient Sir John Crooke
and read his message in his book.*

*Very well, Said Sir William Morris, So
But Henry Ludlowe's tail cried No*

*Up starts one fuller of devotion
then Eloquence; and said a very ill motion*

Not so neither say Sir Henry Jenkin,
the Motion was good; but for the stinking

Well said Sir Henry Poole it was a bold trick
to fart in the nose of the body politic

I must confess said Sir Edward Grevill
the matter of it self was somewhat uncivil

Thank God said Sir Edward Hungerford
that this Fart proved not a Turd

Said Sir Jerome the less there was no such abuse
ever offered in Poland, or Spruce

Said Sir Jerome in folio, I swear by the Masse
this Fart was enough to have broke all my Glass

Indeed said Sir John Trevor it gave a foul knock
as it launched forth from his stinking dock.

I (said another) it once so chanced
that a great man farted as he danced.

Well then, said Sir William Lower
this fart is no Ordinance fit for the Tower.

Said Sir Richard Houghton no Justice of Quorum
but would take it in snuff to have a fart let before him.

If it would bear an action said Sir Thomas Holcroft
I would make of this fart a shaft or a bolt

Said Sir Walter Cope 'twas a fart rarely let
I would 'tweere sweet enough for my Cabinet.

Such a Fart was never seen
said the learned Counsel of the Queen.

No said Mr. Pecke I have a President in store
that his Father farted the Session before

Nay then said Noy 'twas lawfully done
for this fart was entail'd from father to son

Said Mr. Recorder a word for the city
to cut of the aldermen's right were great pity.

Well said Kit Brookes we give you a reason
though he has right by descent he had not livery & seizing

Ha ha said Mr. Evans I smell a fee
it's a private motion here's something for me

Well said Mr. Moore lets this motion repeal,
what's good for the private is oft ill for commonweal

A good year on this fart, said gentle Sir Harry
he has caused such an earthquake that my colepitts miscarry

'Tis hard to recall a fart when its out
Said with a loud shout

The World Famous French Farting Man

Joseph Pujol (1857-1945) discovered early in life that he had one special skill that no one else seemed to posses. He was able to breath in air through his anus and fart it back out again at will.

Taking the stage name Le Petomane (French for Fart-o-Maniac), the Frenchman refined this unique talent into a stage act and toured the world. Everywhere he went he wowed the crowds by using his amazing ass to blow out candles, play the flute, and even smoke cigarettes, all with apparently odorless emissions.

His act would begin with a comedic series of 'fart impressions'. First he would let off a tiny little pop, which he playfully referred to as the "the fart of a new bride", then he would let off an thunderously earth shaking butt rumble which he labeled as "the same bride a week into the marriage".

For his finale Le Pétomane would insert a rubber tube into his backside, and attach an ocarina to the end of the hose. He would then play the popular tunes of the day while inviting his audience to join in the sing along.

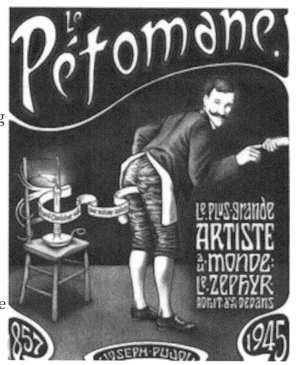

He was a great success at the Moulin Rouge and eventually opened his own theatre. At one point his remarkable skill ended up making the highest paid and most famous entertainer in all of France.

Joseph Pujol passed away in 1945 at the age of eighty-eight. After his death his family were inundated with requests from medical schools in Paris that wanted to examine his famous anus. Unfortunately for science his family declined their requests, saying simply that 'there are some things in this life which simply must be treated with reverence,' *(and clearly a musical butt is one of them).*

Adolf Hitler's deadly farts

Adolf Hitler has a reputation for being one crazy dude (and not in a good way), but could his butt gas situation have helped to push him totally over the edge? According to medical reports Hitler suffered from extremely painful and persistent gas; an agonising condition which led to constant uncontrollable farting.

Naturally suffering from incessant bottom burps isn't the kind of thing that makes the average murderous dictator all that happy, so in his desperate search for a cure he began to take medications containing strychnine and Atropene.

While Hitler's anti-gas pills, contained non-lethal amounts of the poisons he kept upping the dose. By the time Hitler was invading the Soviet Union in early 1941, he was reportedly popping between 120 to 150 pills a week. Trouble is strychnine and Atropene tend to make one rather tense and edgy, and they are known to cause insomnia, which can in turn lead to madness.

While no one really knows what role Hitler's fart pills played in the horrendous murderous rampage that was WW2, but some historians have speculated that things may have not have been so bad were it not for Hitler's chronically painful bum blasts.

As a foot note, according to his biographer, it was Hitler's desperation to get some relief from his flatulence that led him to become a vegetarian. (Clearly he never spent too much time with bean munching hippies!)

Fart Jokes

Fart Jokes come in all shapes and sizes. There are the long form story type, question and answer jokes, limericks, sound gags, sight gags, there is in fact no type of joke in which a fart can't figure. Of course some fart jokes are absolutely hilarious, some are funny and some are... well... total stinkers!

Q: What is it called when the Queen farts?
A: A noble gas.

Q: What's the definition of bravery?
A: A man with diarrhea chancing a fart!

Q: What is the definition of surprise?
A: A fart with a lump in it.

Q: Why do farts stink?
A: So that deaf people can enjoy them also!

Q: What do you call a person that doesn't fart in public?
A: A private Toot-er.

Q: What do you call a cat who likes to eat beans?
A: Puss n Toots.

Q: What's the difference between a museum and Mr. Methane?

A: One has artifacts; the other does farty acts.

Q: What's the difference between Mozart and Mr. Methane?

A: One is music to your ear; the other is music from his rear.

Q: What is Green and Smelly?

A: The Hulk's farts.

Q: What do you get if you eat refried beans and onions?

A: Tear Gas.

Q: How can you tell if a woman is wearing pantyhose?

A: Her ankles swell when she farts.

Q: Why don't little girls fart?

A: Because they don't have an ass until they get married.

Q: What is the sharpest thing in the world?

A: A Fart. It goes through your pants and doesn't even leave a hole.

Q: Why don't you fart in church?

A: Because you have to sit in your pew.

Q: What do you call "fart" in German?

A: Farfrompoopin!

The elevator

A very poor old lady was taking the elevator to her doctor's office, which was in a rather swanky upmarket building. The elevator stopped and a rich young woman got on smelling of heavily of perfume. The young women glared at the poor old lady thinking she just didn't belong in such a lovely, upmarket building. But the old woman just smiled and inhaled deeply saying "that's a lovely perfume you have". The young woman snapped back at the old lady, "Yes, it's Romance by Ralph Lauren and it costs $150.00, an ounce!"

A few floors up the elevator stopped again and another young woman got on also smelling heavily of perfume. She also glared disapprovingly at the poor old woman. The old woman smiled and just sniffed her perfume. The second woman also snapped back at her, "that's Chanel#5, and it's worth $200.00 an ounce!"

About 3 floors later, the elevator stopped and the old woman went to get out, but before she left, she bent over and let off a massively stinky butt blaster. She turned back and glared at the snobby women and simply said "Broccoli 99 cents a pound!"

Three Pilots

Three pilots, a Mexican, a Japanese and an American where taking turns flying over each of their countries. As they flew over Japan the Japanese pilot dropped on apple on her country. The two other pilots asked he why she did that and she said, "because I love my country".

Next they flew over Mexico and the Mexican dropped an orange on his country. When asked why he did that and he said, "Because I love my country".

They continued on to fly over America and the American dropped a bomb on his country. Surprised the other two asked him why he did that and he said, "Because I hate my country"

Eventually when they landed in their respective countries the Japanese pilot was walking and she saw a kid crying and asked her what the matter was. The kid told her an apple fell out of the sky and hit me in the head.

Then the Mexican was walking and he saw a kid crying so he asked what happened and the kid said "an orange fell out of the sky and hit him in the head".

Then the American was walking and he saw a kid laughing and he ask what are you so happy about and he said "I farted and the building behind me exploded"

Teacher Teacher

A teacher asked little Tommy to use the word "definitely " in a sentence. To which Tommy replied, "Teacher, do farts have lumps in them?" The Teacher said, "Oh don't be silly Tommy, of course not," To which Tommy replied, "Oh, well in that case I have definitely pooped my pants."

The Question

A boy rushes home from school and announces to his parents "Mom, dad, the teacher asked a question today and I was the only kid in the class that knew the answer!" His parents puff up with pride and say "Why that's amazing son! What was the question?" And the boy says "Who farted?"

The Restaurant

A woman walks into a restaurant and takes a seat. As she bends down to reach into her purse for her wallet, she lets off a thunderous cheek slapper, with the Waiter right behind her. Shocked and embarrassed, she quickly sits back up and looks around to see everyone staring at her. Thinking quickly she attempts to divert blame away from herself by glaring directly at the waiter and shouting "Stop That!" To which the Waiter replies "Sure, which way did it go?"

Bill and Ben

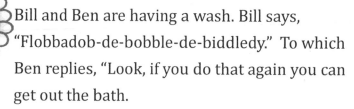

Bill and Ben are having a wash. Bill says, "Flobbadob-de-bobble-de-biddledy." To which Ben replies, "Look, if you do that again you can get out the bath.

Farting in Bed

A man silently farted in bed and slowly lifted up the quilt. After a few seconds his wife screamed loudly, "OMG Dave, that stinks!"...It must've been pretty awful, she was downstairs at the time!

The Bet

A man was sitting on the sofa with his wife when a hideous smell permeated the room. "Phew" She said holding her nose, "what's that smell, have you farted?" The husband looked coyly at her and said, "No I haven't". She said, "I bet you fifty dollars that you have".

"Ok" said the husband, "it's a bet". He then pulled down his pants and showed them to his wife. "See" he said, "it wasn't a fart, that will be fifty dollars please!"

Farting Dixie

A scruffy hobo walks into a bar and orders a whiskey. The bartender eyes him suspiciously and says, "I'll have to see your money first." The hobo smiles and says "You got me, I'm broke. But I tell you what, if you give me a bottle of whiskey, I'll get up on that stage and fart Dixie!"

The bartender was intrigued. He had never seen anyone fart a tune, and so he agrees. The hobo chugs down the whole bottle of whiskey, then staggers up on stage and drops his pants. The audience starts applauding wildly. The hobo then proceeds to poops all over the stage. Totally disgusted and everyone leaves. The bartender screams, "You said you were going fart Dixie! Not poop all over my stage!" The hobo replies, "Hey! Every singer has to clear his throat before he sings!"

The iPhone Debacle

A man wanders into a coffee shop enjoying the music from his iphone... Suddenly realizes he needs to fart. To cover his tracks he ups the volume thinking 'yes, the music is loud enough so no one will hear me' so he closes his eyes and lets go of one long loud squelchy bubbling blurt... When he opens his eyes again everyone is staring at him. Then he realizes, he was wearing headphones!

The Church Pew

An elderly couple head out to church early on a Sunday morning, halfway through the reverend's most serious sermon the wife leans over and whispers to her husband, "I've just let out a silent fart. What should I do?" The husband replies, "Put a new battery in your hearing aid."

Fido

A man takes his new girlfriend to dinner at his parents' house for the first time. Of course she is very nervous and desperately wants to make a good impression. Halfway through the wonderful meal, his girlfriend starts to feel a little gas pain building up, (partly due to her nervousness and partly due to the broccoli casserole). It gets worse and worse to the point that the pain is just about making her eyes water.

Left with no other choice, she decides to release a little bit of the pressure and lets out a dainty little fart. It wasn't loud, but everyone at the table heard the gentle poot.

Before she even had a chance to be embarrassed, her boyfriend's father looked over at the dog that had been snoozing at the women's feet, and said in a rather stern voice, "Fido!"

The woman thought, "this is great!" and a big smile came across her face. A couple minutes later, she was beginning to feel the pain again. This time, she didn't even hesitate, and let rip with a long loud juicy one. The father again looked at the dog and yelled, "Dammit Fido!"

Once again the woman smiled and thought, "Yes!" A few minutes later another she felt another one building up a head of steam.. This time she didn't even think about it, and another roaring butt belch came billowing out. Again, the father looked at the dog with disgust and yelled, "Dammit, Fido, get away from her before she poops on you!"

Farty one liners

A skeleton was trying to fart in a crowded place. But in the end it couldn't because it had no guts.

Why fart and waste when you can burp and taste?

A man never really knows just how much he farts until he spends 24 hours with a girl he likes.

You know, one time I farted so badly that I had to spend 15 years in jail.... for air pollution.

I fart... Why? Because it's the only gas I can afford.

I had three oak barrels of wine in my cellar and I just went down there to open up and vent one. It stinks down there now.

While at a fancy dinner party a man farts. Another man says "How dare you fart in front of my wife". The first man says "Sorry, I didn't realize it was her turn".

Did you hear about the constipated Wheel of Fortune player?
He wanted to buy a bowel.

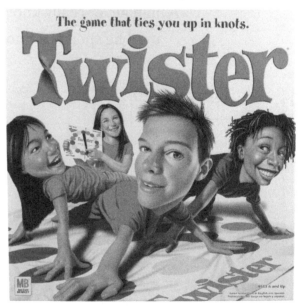

If you fart during a game of Twister, you are dead to me.

Fart Poems and Limericks

There once was a lady from China
Who's pitching just couldn't be finer,
She was able to fart
The violin part
Of a string quartet in A-minor.

A loving young husband called Fred
Put a cork up his backside in bed
Cause his farts had such force
They'd be grounds for divorce
And he wants to stay happily wed.

A fart is just a gust of wind
that cometh from the heart
but if it takes a downward trend
it turns into a fart

There was a young girl who was flustered
Cause she couldn't stop cutting the mustard
She let out a chirp
When her bottom would burp
Hoping she wouldn't get busted

An impressive old man from Sparta
Had incredible skill as a farter
After eating one bean
He'd fart God Save the Queen'
and Beethoven's 'Moonlight Sonata'

There was a young student called Jules
Who couldn't stop breaking the rules
He bought farting jackasses
To all of his classes
And stunk out the school with his mules

A young altar boy called Elias
Let off farts that would constantly try us
The air he would vent
Had a unholy scent
But his backside refused to be pious

That jolly old Greek Aristotle
Gave his wife a fart in a bottle
The smell was so foul
It made his wife scowl
And run from the room at full throttle

There was a young lady called Shelly
Who had gaseous pains in her belly
When wind she did pass
With a thunderous blast
Her farts where exceedingly smelly

There once was a man called Rory
Who went on trial in Missouri
His farted so hard
His backside was scarred
And he got sent away by the Jury

There once was a lady called June
Who farted a merry old tune
She'd smile and she'd say
She took pride in the way
The mist from her rump filled the room

A talented man from Jakarta
Was known as a musical farter
The first blast from his bum
Would equal a drum
And bugle notes followed thereafter

A handsome young swimmer called Bart
Said I win every race by a fart
I breakfast on beans
till I'm full to the seams
Then I race jet propelled from the start

Farting Romeos

As a rule you could say that farting isn't really a part of the language of love, with both sexes trying their hardest not to fart when dating. It has even been said that one never really knows just how much they fart until they spend a full day with someone they really like! After all, trying not to fart on a date can be total agony.

But believe it or not there are some people out there that think a good fart gag will actually help them get a date. The fact that people are rarely, if ever, romantically swept off their feet by a good rump shaking trouser puff is well known, but some true believers refuse to be swayed by reason.

If you want to try your hand at igniting a romance with a quick quip about a mystical butt cheek bubbler, you might consider giving one of these tried and true pick up lines a go.

*Did you fart, because you just blew me away?

*Mind if I hang out here until its safe back where I farted?

*Hey, somebody farted. Let's get out of here.

*I didn't fart. My intestines just blew you a kiss.

Why we fart

Every one farts, no exception. Mums, dads, sisters, brothers, kings, queens, doctors, teachers, lawyers, pop stars, Kim Kardashian, absolutely everyone. It is in fact quite normal for the average person to push out around half a gallon (2 liters) of stink gas a day. That is enough puff to pop off about 15 to 20 toots. But where does all this gas come from?

Firstly there is the air that we swallow whenever we munch on anything. That air has to come out somewhere and unless you are a keen belcher, well let's just say it's got to make it's way to the other exit.

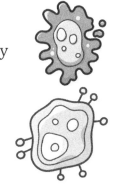

Then there are the colonies of gut bacteria that are responsible for those really ripe smelly little devils. (Yes the ones that send your family reeling). When these magic little microbes set to work processing a meal they not only extract all the nutrients we need from our food, they produce a stinkerific gaseous byproduct call hydrogen sulphide. Hydrogen sulphide is also responsible for the fetid stench we get off rotten eggs, (and quite bizzarly hydrogen sulphide gives male rats an erection... which means male rats actually get all romantic when they smell a fart).

Without our gut bacteria making its lovely smells we couldn't extract any nutrients from our food. Which means everyone has to fart to survive, and if you don't fart you'll die! So next time you peel off a ripe one remember, you fart to live!

That said everyone has different combinations of bacteria in their intestines and everyone one eats slightly different combinations of food. This is what leads to the wide range of backside perfumes. Depending on your combination of gut bacteria and what you have been munching your gas may be sweet as rose petals or you may be able to clear a room with a single puff.

Of course some foods will bring on more volume and more stench than others. But it's not just the usual suspects. There are many culprits that are not broadly known and therefore don't have the wafty reputation they deserve. If you really want to give yourself lots of gas to stink up the place there are plenty of farty foods for you to pick from:

Sitting on top on the league-table of fart makers are sugars. Sugars are the undisputed champion big guns. Just as sugars ferment to make alcohol, sugars also ferment to make massively grand farts.

The biggest sugary culprits are:

Fructose — Fructose is a natural fruit sugar. It is added to just about all sweet (and some not so sweet) junk foods. Fructose occurs naturally in most fruits and some vegetables like onions and corn, and even in some grains like wheat. It is often concentrated down into a sugary syrup which is used in the manufacture of soft drinks.

Lactose — Lactose is the name for the natural sugars that occur in dairy products. Lactose is often added to breads and cereals. Some people have very low levels of "lactase" which is an enzyme that breaks down lactose in their system.

People who have low levels of lactase are sometimes called lactose intolerant. These poor people tend to let off unbelievable clouds of toe curling stink gas when they eat dairy, or any other product high in lactose.

Raffinose — Raffinose is what is called a trisaccharide. Which put simply means a sugar that is made up of three other sugars, in this case galactose, glucose and fructose.

Unlike cows and other ruminants that have two chambers to their stomachs, animals with only one stomach (monogastrics) such as humans don't have the a-gal enzyme that is needed to breakdown raffinose. So when humans consume raffinose it passes through to the lower intestine undigested, where it is fermented by the gut's bacteria to make carbon dioxide, methane or hydrogen.

Raffinose is commonly found in many vegetables, including asparagus, beans, broccoli, cabbage and cauliflower.

Sorbitol —Sorbitol is an indigestible sugar that is found in most fruits. It is also used in "diet" and sugar-free foods as an artificial sweetener. While sorbitol may be lower in calories than other sugars it is none the less great for filling up that high-pressure gas pipe down below.

Fart Making Foods:

Of course no-one eats sugars on their own. They always come wrapped up in some food or another. If you want to brew up a stink wild enough to knock out your grandma you might want to try some of these fab fart foods:

Fruit: Particularly apples (yes there was a good reason God told Adam not to touch the apple tree), apricots, bananas, grapes, melons, peaches, pears, plums, prunes and raisins.

Beans: After sugars comes the most well known of culprits; beans. Yes beans, beans, beans, all kinds of beans; navy beans, red beans, pinto beans, lima beans, garbanzo beans, aduki beans and lentils just to name a few. If you want to toot like a champion beans are definitely the go.

Cruciferous Vegetables:
Cruciferous vegetables are plants such as broccoli, cauliflower, cabbage and Brussels sprouts. These veggies make some people blow up like a hot air balloon, and there is only one way to relieve that kind of pressure.

Dairy Products: Did you know cows are some of the biggest farters on the planet? In fact the methane released in cow farts makes up more of the totel global greenhouse gasses than cars. Given their status as one of the world's biggest emitters of backside methane it's no surprise that diary is a major contributor to human flatulence.

If your gut is a bit sensitive to dairy, eating a cheeseburger can lead to some of the most vile and heinous butt stink you will encounter. In fact someone who is particularly lactose intolerant could render an entire movie theatre uninhabitable with a single ripe dairy bomb.

Oat Bran: Yes there is a reason that little orphan Oliver asked for more porridge. Living with all those boys it was a not stop fart-athon, and he needed plenty of fuel on board to be in the competition.

Soda: Let us not forget soda. Fizzy drinks, especially those with high fructose corn syrup are a sure fire way to let off a few crackers.

Other fart-forming champions include the fibre and starches found in foods like corn, wheat, peas, nuts, barley, bulgar and potatoes.

While proteins and fats don't directly cause gas themselves, they can slow down digestion, which can give your bevy of bacteria more time to generate their magical fragrances from the other ingredients in your meal.

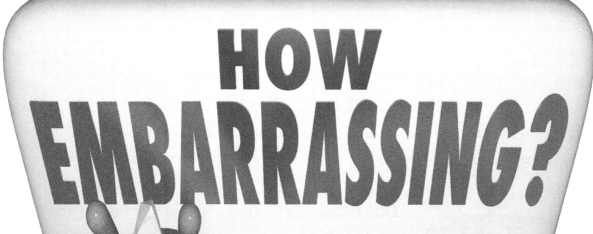

HOW EMBARRASSING?

— 100% SHAME

— DISCOMFORT

— REGRETFUL

— BLUSHING

Fart Fixes

In spite of the fact that the humble fart is hilariously funny and endlessly entertaining, popping off can actually be a problem for some people. For example, for some inexplicable reason girls often don't like to fart, and if they do they often don't want to admit it. Girls are often looking for ways to avoid pumping gas (especially in public).

There are of course many times in life when it is better not to fart, such as meeting the Queen, or getting married, or going for a job interview. Keeping it in for such occasions can be a real struggle if you are keen and frequent butt honker, but you can reduce your chances of accidently blowing your horn at an inopportune moment.

If your bottom is causing you trouble by belching like a champion at all the wrong times and in all the wrong places you might want to try some of these proven remedies for your uncontrolled rump rippers:

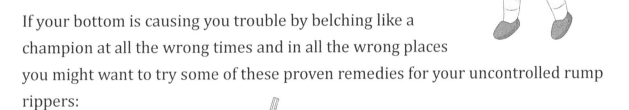

Eliminate the culprits: Pretty simple really, if it makes you pop, it's time to stop. Just don't eat it. This is easier said than done, and of course you must work out what it is that is making you break wind. If you think you know what is causing all the rampant butt yodeling then that is a good place to start. Simply cut the suspect food out of your diet for one to two weeks. If the pops stop, problem solved!

If you seem to be tooting non stop and have no idea exactly which foods are having a blast in your intestines, you might want to try stopping all the fart foods on the list and slowly test each one until you find the offending item.

Cut down on the portion size: Of course if cheese is your wind breaking nemesis, and you just love eating cheese more than anything, then stopping altogether may be a big ask. There is however a good chance that you may be able to have a little Cheddar now and again without going the nuclear trouser trumpet. The trick is to try eating just a little, wait about four to eight hours and see what happens. You may find that there is safe amount you can eat.

Get some enzyme action: This doesn't work on everyone but it is worth a shot. There are a number of over-the-counter products such as "Beano" that you can buy that contain the alpha-galactosidase enzyme, which will break down some of the foods we can't digest efficiently. Enzyme supplements such as Lactaid are also worth trying if you are lactose intolerant. Digestive supplements may not allow you to eat the offending food in large quantities, but they would probably allow you to down the odd bean nachos without blowing the house down.

Avoid swallowing air: Chewing gum while drinking soda pop may indeed be a popular pastime, but it is sure fire way to gas up your stomach. If you want to keep the air clear, it is best avoid them.

Other air gulping activities include talking while you eat and stuffing too much food into your gob at once. So keep it quiet and take manageable mouthfuls if you want to avoid cutting the cheese in public.

Release the pressure valve: Once you have a full tank on board, there is nothing you can do but release your fumes. Thankfully there are a couple of options that don't necessarily involve gassing everyone in the room.

Gas Relievers: For a start you could try a "gas reliever" such as "Gas-X", which contains simethicone (an ingredient that reduces the surface tension of gas bubbles so that they leave your system more easily).

Go the herbal hippie: If you'd like to calm the thunder down under in a natural holistic way you could try some of Mother Earth's finest herbal remedies. Cardamom, ginger, fennel, peppermint, pumpkin and yoghurt are known for their ability to treat uncontrollable ass clapping.

Go Pro: Some people swear by using probiotics (beneficial good gut bacteria, like those found in yoghurt) to reduce their stink reserves, although you should proceed with caution as probiotics can actually increase gassiness in some people.

Try Yoga! Yes seriously! Those hippies really know how to work up some wildly pungent bottom vapours with all those beans and lentils, so it should come as no surprise that the happy hippy pastime of yoga could help with such a pressing problem. To clear the pipes fast, try striking the "wind releasing" yoga pose:

Lie flat on your back and take a deep breath. Lift your left leg and bend your knee, drawing it slowly up to your chest. Placing your hands over that knee pull it gently

toward you. Lift your head off the floor and bring your forehead toward your bent knee. Hold for a moment, then lower your head back to the floor and straighten your leg until you are lying flat on your back again. Repeat with the right leg. Do a set of three on each side. Breathe slowly and deeply throughout the pose. Repeat as often as needed.

If bubbling bloats persist in spite of your best efforts you may want to go and see your doctor. It could be a simple side effect of a basic medications (such as aspirin, antacids or narcotic pain relievers, multivitamins, iron pills etc.)…or it could be sign that there is an underlying medical problem such as Irritable Bowel Syndrome.

Let it rip: Whatever you do don't make a habit of holding in a noxious air biscuit! According to recent studies published in the New Zealand Medical Journal, holding back your gas can cause heartburn, bloating, indigestion and acute pain. Trapped gas can also lead to intestinal distension and an increase in blood pressure and heart rate; so for the sake of your good health, free that booty belch!

Seriously though: While farts are natural and fun if there are other symptoms, it is time to go and see the doctor. If you have constipation or diarrhea that won't go away, an unexplained weight loss, Chronic abdominal bloating and pain, blood in your poo, or if you have a high temperature, muscle pains, vomiting, chills, and other signs of infection.

Bottom Blast Etiquette - To Fart or not to fart?...

Are you a little active on the gas pump? Is your farty behind is costing you friendships or relationships?

Nature can be so cruel. Sometimes you really just need to push out the California barking spider, but it's not always the polite thing to do. While some people will give a gleeful giggle, others will take great offence at the tiniest toot. Of course holding it in isn't always an option so what is one to do?

In this section we are going to take a look at some of the real life fart situations you might find your self in.

The Elevator:

It can be a tough call, when the pressure builds up in a crowded elevator. The first thing you have to do is work out whether it is going to be an SBD or a loud and proud. If you can be sure it will be silent you are probably safe to drop your load, but if it is going to roar like a lion it might be better to push the button and jump out at the next floor, (that is if you can hold it that long).

The Dinner Table:

If you feel the need to let loose at home that is one thing, but when you are out in restaurant or at friends house for dinner then that is another thing all together. If you have the time, excuse your self and get to the bathroom quick sticks. Even if you totally stink out the bathroom no one will call you on it, however if you let it rip at the table you can expect at least a raised eyebrow or two.

Hopefully your popper won't take you by surprise but if you are caught out at a friends house, you can always blame the dog, or in an emergency the cat. If your

hosts are polite they won't make a big thing of calling you out on it.

The Job Interview:

This is simple, if you want the job, no beans for at least two days before hand. If you don't want the job, scoff down those bean tacos like there is no tomorrow. Trust me on this, if you go in there tooting like steam engine there is no way you are starting on Monday.

The Big Date:

Same as the job interview really. If you actually like your date, try and keep the pipes clear for a few days prior, but if you are forced out on a date with your parent's friend's unlikable nerd spawn then by all means practice the backyard bugle all night long.

If you do happen to let a fog horn slip though in front of your latest crush, then you can always try and cover by saying "Wow, we must have a real connection, I don't usually feel comfortable enough to do that on a date" ... I admit this is a pretty lame attempt at a save, but you did just fart in front of that special someone!!!

Farting in an Airplane:

If you are on a flight you are going to fart, that is just he nature of air travel. The lower level or air pressure in the cabin causes more gas bubbles to form in your gut, which can naturally only lead to one thing.

If you are on a quick commuter flight it is usually not too much of a problem, but if you are on a long haul then it can get a bit odorous.

If you are regular farty pants try and get an aisle seat so you can dash to the bathroom as needed, but if you are not expecting too much turbulence on the flight you are probably safe to take a window seat.

NO FARTING NO FARTING NO FARTING

Farting around the world

Farting may be universal but our relationship with flatulence certainly is not. While many cultures frown on letting one rip over dinner, others do not. For example, while you are considered grossly rude if you belch in a restaurant in Japan, it is said to be perfectly fine to let off a honkingly loud ass toot.

And it's not just the Japanese that appreciate a well tune rectal puff. It turns out that the Inuit people of Canada think farting after a meal is an expression of thanks and appreciation. (Surely that can't be true?)

Fart Shame?

Fart shame is not a laughing matter. It can in fact be deadly serious. Take the sobering case of Marc Higgins for example. Few people in history have been so especially shamed by their farts as Mr. Higgins, from England. One Friday night as he was casually enjoying a party with his friends he reportedly let loose with one seriously savage subterranean snarl. The other partygoers were quite naturally overcome by his noxious nasal offering and proceeded to mock him mercilessly for his odorous affront.

Higgins responded in the way any totally insane, irrational maniac might; by storming from the party, only to return later and start indiscriminately stabbing people in a misguided effort to teach them a lesson in courtesy.

In total, Higgins stabbed four people, killing one, just because they made fun of his farts. He eventually turned himself in stating he didn't mean to do it, he just wanted them to not mock him.

So, a word to the wise, before you mock someone's fart you better make sure they can take the pressure.

Farting At The Movies

There was a time when farting in films just wasn't done. Fortunately that rule was blown away in 1971 by a little known film called "Cold Turkey" starring Dick Van Dyke and Bob Newhart. The film was by all accounts a bit of Turkey itself, and failed to impress at the box office, but nonetheless its place in history was secured as the film that broke the film farting taboo, paving the way for such classic cinema moments like the notorious Blazing Saddles campfire scene.

Here is a quick list of the all time best and funniest "smelluloid" farts...

Blazing Saddles (1974): Mel Brooks brings us possibly the first, and one of the greatest movie fart scenes of all times, the cowboys eating baked beans around the camp fire scene. Possibly one of the longest fart scenes in cinema history and certainly the one with most people actively farting.

Amadeus (1984): Does Mozart really fart at his audience in this movie? Yes, yes he does, and I must say it is pretty funny.

Spies Like Us (1985): While boning up on his spy skills Chevy Chase drops a quick side blast in class.

The Garbage Pail Kids Movie (1987): This has one of the most epic farts in the history of cinema, blowing away an entire audience.

Naked Gun (1988): After speaking at a conference the lead character Frank Drebin excuses himself and heads off to use the bathroom, unfortunately he forgets to take his microphone off. The tinkling sound of his peeing can be heard by everyone... and then to top it all off nicely he rips a big one!

Dances with Wolves (1990): Proving that even Academy Award winning films can have fireside fart jokes.

Dumb and Dumber (1994): There are a couple of topnotch fart moments in this movie. The first is when Lloyd spikes Harry's drink with a laxative. When Harry sits down to relieve himself he practically explodes, and the noises are, well, quite funny. After he is done he finishes it all up with quite a nice little toot.

The other great fart scene is when Lloyd is thinking about Mary at a winter party. Lloyd performs his best party trick by lifting his legs over his head and farting into a cigarette lighter. Naturally it lights up like a blowtorch.

The Nutty Professor (1996): Eddie Murphy is no stranger to the big screen fart gag, and this one is no exception, featuring a veritable fart festival over the dinner table.

Beavis and Butt-Head Do America (1996): Being an animation they had no trouble putting together atomic bomb of a nuclear butt blast.

Austin Powers – International Man of Mystery (1997): In this immortal cinema classic Mike Myers hops in the tub for his own special kind of bubble bath.

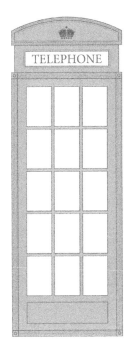

Spawn (1997): Who could resist the urge to crack up when a huge puff of green butt gas seeps out of an Alien backside? It's a quick gag but a goody!

Rocket Man (1997): This classic is one of the only films in which you can find the thing most feared by all astronauts… "a fart in a space suit".

Rain Man (1998): Dustin Hoffman lets loose a deadly air biscuit while in a phone booth with Tom Cruise.

South Park – Bigger Longer & Uncut (1999): More squelching butt antics from those whacky Canadian South Park characters Terrance and Phillip; is anyone surprised by this?

Love Stinks (1999): While the title doesn't lead a lot to the imagination, farting in bed is still totally hilarious, even if you know it's coming.

Mystery Men (1999): This somewhat weird superhero movie features a character called "The Spleen". The Spleen's super power is quite literally in his butt. Whether it is blasting people with his sonic ass cheeks or choking them with an SBD (silent but deadly), this movie is one nonstop fart gag.

Shrek (2001): Shrek was probably the first and certainly the most famous animated character to let one rip on screen. His stinky blasts proving so popular that it's now taken for granted Shrek is going to peel one off in every movie he is in.

Click (2007): While it is not recommended that you try this at home, in this little flick Adam Sandler squats on a desk and farts directly in someones face. How could it fail to be funny?

Step Brothers (2008): With Will Ferrell and John C Reilly star in this outrageous comedy cast as, yep you guessed it, stepbrothers!
John C Reilly's character lets rip with one of the longest on screen farts ever, clocking in at massive 14 seconds.

Police Academy: There a lot of police academy movies and they all pay homage to the fart joke, so it doesn't matter which one you pick they are all fart festivals from start to finish.

The Swiss Army Man (2016): This questionable comedy begins with a dead body played by Daniel Radcliff (AKA Harry Potter) washing up on a beach.
When a crazed castaway inspects the body, it breaks wind and twitches. The castaway befriends the farting corpse and thus the movie unfolds. This film is by all accounts totally gross, but any movie that stars a farting corpse is worth a mention.

Arty Farty – The Farts in High Art

From paintings to sculpture to great works of literature the humble fart has a long and illustrious history when it comes to the arts. Believe it or not farts have figured in some pretty major artworks.

The Japanese farting scrolls:

He-Gassen - a.k.a. "the fart war."

During Japan's Edo period (approximately 200-400 years ago), an unknown Japanese artist created one of the finest tributes to flatulence ever produced in the history of art.

The "farting scrolls" are a series of complex and engaging artworks, in which both men and women are depicted taking aim and shooting humungous torrents of backside gas at each other.

Not just a mere celebration of rectal turbulence, the scrolls are said to be a form of political satire designed to express Japanese displeasure with a rising tide of European cultural influence. This political fart artist would even depict Westerners being blown home on thunderous blasts of rump mist.

From a Japanese scroll, titled "He-Gassen"—translated as "Fart Battle"
dated approx. 1846

Medieval Art Farts

Did you know that medieval devotional books where full of fart jokes? Back in the days before the printing press was invented books used to be hand made by especially skilled scribes. Alongside the text these books were filled with exquisitely detailed drawings, known today as marginalia.

These books where usually commissioned by wealthy educated elites who seemed to enjoy nothing more than a good dose of poop humor with their bible studies. It is not uncommon to see farting animals, or little angels blowing backside trumpets in the margins of medieval holy books.

The Farting Bull

The farting bull sculpture is one of the most stunning examples of flatulance in modern art. Chinese artist Chen Wenling's explosive sculpture is so large it took a whole gallery to dispay it, so while it is one truly amazing piece of installation art, I am not sure if anyone could fit into their lounge room.

Apparently it is Chen Wenling's statement on unchecked greed. It depicts a massive fart launching the golden bull of wall street into the air and pinning a demon-horned Bernie Madoff (the disgraced hedge fund manager who stole millions of dollars of is client's money) to a wall.

It was exhibited at the Bejiing Art Gallery in 2009.
Seriously no bull!

The Great Farts of Literature

Did you know that some of the greatest works literary works in history are filled to the brim with ripping good fart jokes? Which just goes to show you, even some of the greatest writers in history couldn't resist the temptation to pop in a few poots when pumping out a cracking yarn.

The Fart Jokes of William Shakespeare

Shakespeare was a great lover of the fart gag, and worked one into many of his plays. Even though it can be a bit hard to spot them at first (as Shakespearean English is a bit out of date now), I am sure his malodourous offerings where considered quite hysterical when first performed at the Globe Theater in Elizabethan England.

King Lear

In King Lear, the king gives a speech as his daughter is thrown out into a storm:
"Blow, winds, and crack your cheeks! Rage, blow!"

Of course, one could argue that Shakespeare was just saying the wind was blowing… but given how much he like a fart joke, I'm sure he meant it to have a double meaning.

The Comedy of Errors

In The Comedy of Errors, a character named Dromio says:

"A man may break a word with you, sir, and words are but wind
Ay, and break it in your face, so he break it not behind".

What Dromio is actually saying here is that it is better to have someone lie to you than fart at you... Oh Shakespeare, you are a crack up!

Othello

In Othello, musicians are performing when a clown interrupts them.

CLOWN: *Are these, I pray you, wind instruments?*

FIRST MUSICIAN: *Ay marry are they, sir*

CLOWN: *O, thereby hangs a tail.*

FIRST MUSICIAN: *Whereby hangs a tail, sir?*

CLOWN: *Marry, sir, by many a wind instrument that I know.*

By "tail" the clown actually means a butt, and that the butt is a wind instrument and the fart is the music it plays! You have to admit that is one sophisticated gag to find in one of the greatest plays ever written.

Two Gentlemen from Verona

In Two Gentlemen from Verona, a young man named Proteus has a crush on a girl called Silvia. To try and win her favor Proteus gives her a farting dog named Crab.

As a servant named Launce explains:

LAUNCE: *I was sent to deliver [the dog] as a present to Mistress Silvia from my master . . .* (the dog goes under the Duke's table); *he had not been there, bless the mark, a pissing while but all the chamber smelt him.* [Translation: The dog farts.]
'Out with the dog' says one;
'What cur is that?' says another;
'Whip him out' says the third;
'Hang him up' says the Duke. *I, having been acquainted with the smell before, knew it was Crab, and goes me to the fellow that whips the dogs.*

'Friend,' quoth I 'you mean to whip the dog.' 'Ay, marry do I' quoth he.
'You do him the more wrong,' quoth I; ''twas I did the thing you wot of.'
[Translation: "I farted."]

He makes me no more ado, but whips me out of the chamber.

So in this scene the dog did a whopper of a popper and was going to be whipped, but the kind servant Launce took the blame and was whipped instead.

Henry IV, Part 1,

In Henry IV, Part 1, two rebel leaders speak, namely Owen Glendower and Harry Hotspur. Here, Glendower is claiming to be a mighty wizard whose birth was a big deal.

GLENDOWER: *I say the earth did shake when I was born . . . The heavens were all on fire, the earth did tremble.*

HOTSPUR: *O, then the earth shook to see the heavens on fire and not in fear of your nativity.*
Diseased nature oftentimes breaks forth in strange eruptions. Oft the teeming earth is with a kind of colic pinched and vexed by the imprisoning of unruly wind within her womb, which for enlargement striving shakes the old beldam earth and topples down steeples and moss-grown towers. At your birth our grandma earth, having this distemperature, in passion shook.

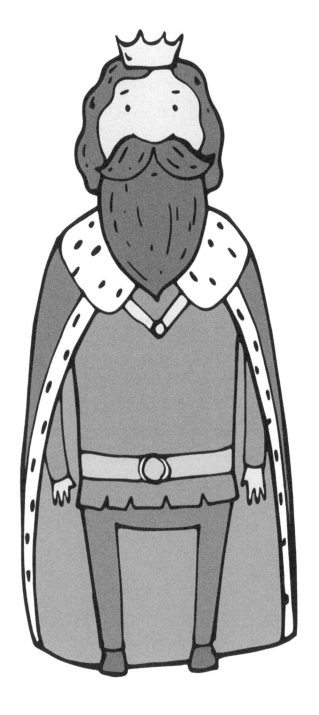

Translation: "The earth farted when you were born."

Dante Alighieri - The Inferno (14th Century CE)

Dante's Inferno is one of the most enduring works of literature ever written, and possibly the first known reference to a "butt trumpet". In his 14th-century masterpiece Dante chronicles a fictional journey through the circles of hell, (purportedly made by Dante himself).

Near the close of chapter XXI, he witnesses a demon mobilizing his troops by using *"his ass as a trumpet."* Now that is a rousing reveille!

Geoffrey Chaucer - The Canterbury Tales (14th Century CE)

In the Miller's Tale Chaucer describes how parish clerk named Absalom was nearly blinded by an impoverished student named Nicholas who inadvertently *"let fly a fart as loud as it had been a thunder-clap, and well nigh blinded Absalom, poor chap."*

Jonathan Swift - "The Benefit of Farting" (1722)

Jonathan Swift, (the author of Gulliver's Travels) penned this infamous essay entitled "The benefit of Farting", thus proving himself to be quite the fart connoisseur. Swift published this lofty work under the pseudonym "Don Fartinando Puff-Indorst, Professor of Bumbast in the University of Crackow."
To quote:

"I take it there are five or six different species of fart." These are *"the sonorous and full-toned or rousing fart," "the double fart," "the soft fizzing fart," "the wet fart,"* and *"the sullen wind-bound fart."*

Ben Johnson – The Alchemist (1610)

The Alchemist is a wonderful comedic story about three con artists who set up shop in a plague-vacated house in London. Disguising themselves as mystics they set out to sell all manner of charms to unsuspecting suckers. But most notably Ben Johnson's famous play actually opens with a fart gag:

Enter Face, in a captain's uniform, with his sword drawn, and Subtle with a vial, quarrelling, and followed by Dol Common.]

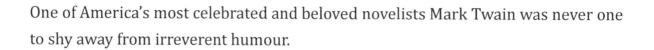

Face: *Believe 't, I will.*
Subtle: *Thy worst. I fart at thee.*

Mark Twain - 1601 (1880)

One of America's most celebrated and beloved novelists Mark Twain was never one to shy away from irreverent humour.

Written in the form of a diary extract from one of Queen Elizabeth I's ladies-in-waiting, "1601" is a fictional account of conversations between the Queen Elizabeth and several famous writers of the day. The topics discussed are entirely scatological, most notably farting.
The diarist describes a conversation in the presence of the queen between various famous Elizabethans during which one of the company farts:

"In ye heat of ye talk it befel yt one did breake wind, yielding an exceding mightie and distresfull stink, whereat all did laugh full sore".

The Queen inquires as to the source, and receives various replies. *"Lady Alice"* and *"Lady Margery"* both deny farting, the first saying:

"Good your grace, an' I had room for such a thundergust

within mine ancient bowels, 'tis not in reason I coulde discharge ye same and live to thank God for yt He did choose handmaid so humble whereby to shew his power. Nay, 'tis not I yt have broughte forth this rich o'ermastering fog, this fragrant gloom, so pray you seeke ye further."

Ben Jonson, Francis Bacon and William Shakespeare (referred to as 'Shaxpur') deny having farted, although they have differing opinions about the merits of the fart. Bacon considers it a *"great performance"* beyond his abilities, and Shakespeare is astounded by its *"firmament-clogging rottenness".*

Walter Raleigh admits to it, but confesses that it was not up to his usual standards, demonstrating his abilities by letting out an even louder one.

Aristophanes - The Clouds (423 BCE)

During the play a rather simple-minded character named Strepsiades gives the famous philosopher Socrates (yes, that Socrates) a little bit too much information about his bowel movements:

"I get colic, then the stew sets to rumbling like thunder and finally bursts forth with a terrific noise. "

James Joyce - Ulysses (1922)

The hero, an advertising salesman called Leopold Bloom, is described in one scene as sitting in a rather unflattering posture: *"asquat the cuckstool... seated calm above his own rising smell."*

1001 Arabian Night's Tales (1709)

In "The Tale of Abu Hassan," Abu is getting married again after his first wife sadly died. Unfortunately for Abu during the wedding celebrations he lets out a fart so raucously loud that he runs away in shame all the way to India where he remains for ten years.

After so many years away he assumes his indiscretion is forgotten and decides to return home. He is just about home when he overhears a mother talking to her daughter.

The daughter is asking when she was born. The mother laughs warmly and replies: *"Thou wast born, my dearest daughter, on the very night that Abu Hasan farted".* Mortified Abu races back to India where he lives in self-exile till he dies.

Wow, talk about an epically embarrassing fart!

John Aubrey - Brief Lives (17th Century CE)

Believe it or not Abu Hassan wasn't the only fictional character to endure a lengthy exile after a devastatingly embarrassing bout of backside trouser tremors.

In his semi-biographical work, Aubrey recounts the following story about the seventeenth Earl of Oxford (1550-1604):

"This Earl... [bowing] to Queen Elizabeth, happened to let a fart, at which he was so abashed and ashamed that he went to travel for seven years". On his return the Queen welcomed him home and said *"My Lord, I had forgotten the fart."*

J.D. Salinger - The Catcher In The Rye (1951)

The character Holden Caulfield is listening to a pompous sermon by a self-aggrandizing minister, when the proceedings are unexpectedly interrupted:

"this guy sitting in the row in front of me, Edgar Marsalla, laid this terrific fart. It was a very crude thing to do, in the chapel and all, but it was also quite amusing. Old Marsalla. He damn near blew the roof off."

Francois Rabelais' - Gargantua and Pantagruel (1532-1545)

Literary Butt Dwarves Anyone?

In Francois Rabelais' Gargantua and Pantagruel, (a five novel work widely considered to be the first ever fantasy epic), a giant rips one so powerful it actually creates little people:

"But with the fart he blew the earth trembled for twenty-seven miles round, and with the fetid air of it he engendered more than fifty-three thousand little men, misshapen dwarfs."

Perhaps a Death Fart Instead?

In the Fifth Book of the series Rabelais also satirised the belief that not farting could cause death. In one story Pantagruel finds himself on the Island where the inhabitants eat nothing but wind and suffer terribly from colic: *"they all fart as they die, the men loudly, the women soundlessly..."*

Here, Rabelais tells the story of a man who quite literally explodes.

"The host had been a sportive fellow in his time, a great lover of good foods, a mighty man for onion soups, a great watcher of the refectory clock, and an eternal diner, like the landlord at Rouillac. Having for the last ten years blown out an abundance of fat, we were told, he had now come to his bursting-time. So, according to the custom of the country, he was ending his days with a burst, since his peritoneum and his skin had been slashed for so many years that they could no longer contain his guts. In fact they could not prevent their pouring out like wine from a burst barrel".

"But tell me, my good people," said Panurge, "couldn't you neatly bind up his belly with good stout girths, or strong hoops of sorb-apple wood, or of iron, if need be? If he were bound up like that he wouldn't throw out his cargo so easily, or burst so soon." Panurge had no sooner finished speaking than we heard a loud, piercing report in the air, as if some mighty oak were splitting in two. Thereupon the neighbours said that the bursting was over, and that this report had been his death-fart.

Benjamin Franklin - The Founding Farter.

One of the great, unpublished works of Benjamin Franklin was an essay he wrote while serving as the US ambassador to France, entitled "Fart Proudly". Apparently Benny was quite proud of his little dissertation and distributed the work widely among his circle of friends, who all thought it was outrageously funny.

But clearly old Ben thought that farting was a matter of the utmost importance, and gave the matter of farting considerable thought. Who knows if he was alive today he may have even come out loudly as a pro fart activist and campaigned to FREE THE FARTS!

It is universally well known, that in the digestion of common food, there is created or produced in the bowels of human creatures, a great quantity of wind. That permitting this air to escape and mix with the atmosphere, is usually offensive to the company, from the fetid smell that accompaniers it.

That all well bred people therefore, to avoid giving such offense, forcibly restrain the efforts of nature to discharge that wind. That so retained contrary to nature, it not only gives frequently great present pain, but occasions future diseases, such as habitual cholics, ruptures, tympanies etc... often distructive of the constitution, and sometimes of life itself.

Where it not for the odiously offensive smell accompanying such escapes, polite people would probably be under no more restraint in discharging such wind in company, than they are in spitting or blowing their noses.

My prize question therefore should be, to discover some drug wholesome and not disagreeable, to be mixed with our common food or sauces that shall render the natural discharges of wind from our bodies not only inoffensive, but agreeable as perfumes.

That this is not a chemical project, and altogether impossible, may appear from these consideration. That we already have some knowledge of means capable of varying that smell. He that dines on stale flesh, especially with the addition of onions shall be able to afford a stink that no company can tolerate, while he that has lived for some time on vegetables only, shall have that breath so pure as to be insensible to the most delicate noses; and if he can manage so as to avoid the report, he may any where give vent to his griefs unnoticed.

But as there are those to whom an entire vegetable diet would be inconvenient, and as a little quick-lime thrown into a Jakes will correct the amazing quantity of fetid stench arising from the vast mass of putrid matter contained in such places, and render it rather pleasing to the smell, who knows but that a little powder of lime (or some other thing equivalent) taken in our food, or perhaps a glass of limewater drank at dinner, may have the same effect on the air produced in and issuing from our bowels? This is worth the experiment.

Certain it is also that we have the power of changing by slight means the smell of another discharge, that of our water. And why should it be thought more impossible in nature, to find means of making a perfume of our wind than of our water?

For the encouragement of this Enquiry, (from the immortal honour to be reasonably expected by the inventor) let it be considered of haw small importance to mankind, or to how small a part of mankind have been useful those discoveries in science that have heretofore made philosophers famous.

Are there twenty men in Europe at this day, the happier, or even the easier , for any knowledge they have picked out of Aristotle?

What comfort can the vortices of Descartes give to a man who has whirlwinds in his Bowels?

The knowledge of Newton's mutual attraction of the particles of matter, can it afford ease to him who is racked by their mutual repulsion and the cruel distensions it occasions?

The pleasure arising to a few philosophers, from seeing , a few times in their life, the threads of light untwisted and separated by the Newtonian prism into seven colours, can it be compared with the ease and comfort of every man might feel seven times a day by discharging freely the wind from his bowels?

Especially if it be converted into a perfume: for the pleasure on one sense being a little inferior to those of another, instead of pleasing the sight he might delight the smell of those about him, and make numbers happy, which to a benevolent mind must afford immediate satisfaction. The generous soul, who now endeavours to find out whether the friends he entertains like best Clartet or Burgundy, Champagne or Madeira, would then enquire also whether they chose musk or lily, rose or bergamot, and provide accordingly. And surely the liberty of expressing one's scent-iments, and pleasing on another, is of infinitely more importance to human happiness than that liberty of the press, or of abusing one another, which the English are so ready to fight and die for.

In short this invention, if completed would be , as Bacon expresses it, bringing philosophy down to men's business and bosoms. And I cannot but conclude, that in comparison there with, for universal continual utility, the science of the philosophers abovementioned, even with the addition, gentlemen of your "figure quelconque" and the figures inscribe in it, are, all together, scarcely worth a FARThing.

Benjamin Franklin 1780

While this may not be totally hilarious by today's standards, I can assure you in 1781 this was absolutely hysterical. Who knew old Ben was such a joker?

A fart by any other name

Shakespeare said, "a rose by any other name would smell as sweet", and the same could be said of your average trouser tickler, but a fart by any other name? Now that can be even funnier! So much so that over the years literally hundreds of terms for farting have infiltrated the English language.

And let's face it; nothing gets the linguistic gymnastics in shape like thinking up new and creative names for a good butt dumpling. It's a fun and totally hilarious pastime.

I have compiled a list of some of the most popular current terms for a good fart. I encourage you to stretch your head, mix and match and come up with as many names for the butt cheek fan as you possibly can.

See if you can work a few into your daily routine and share the sweet scent of your backside love with your friends and family.

A:

Air biscuit, Airbrush your boxers, Air tulip, Anal acoustics, Anal exhale, Anal salute, Anal applause, Anal volcano, Answering the call of the wild burrito, Arkansas barking spider, Ass acoustics, Ass flapper

B:

Backdoor breeze, Back draft, Back-end blowout, Back blast, Baking brownies, Bark, Barking spider, Baking brownies, Barn burner, Bean blower, Beef, Beep your horn,

Belching clown, Benchwarmer, Butt Blast, Blat, Blowing a hottie, Blowing the fog horn, Blowing an ill wind, Blurp, Blurt, Butt Bomber, Butt percussion, Boom-boom, Booty bomb,

Booty cough, Bottom blast, Bottom burp, Booty belch, Break wind, Brown cloud, Brown haze, Brown thunder, Bust ass, Butt cheek bubbler, Butt hair harmony, Butt Putt, Butt trumpet, Buttock bassoon, Bull snort, Bumsen burner, Bung blast, Burner, Burp out the wrong end, Bust ass, Butt bazooka, Butt bongos, Butt cheek screech, Butt dumpling, Butt sneeze, Butt trumpet, Butt tuba, Butt yodelling

C:

California barking spider, Cheek squeaker, Cheeser, Cheese blaster, Cheese cracker, Colon bowlin', Colon power, Cornhole clap, Cornhole tremor, Crack a rat, Crack concert, Crack open the bubbly, Crack splitters, Crack call, Crack Slapper, Cracking an air walnut, Crop dust, Cut loose, Cut the wind, Cut one, Cut the cheese, Cupcake, Cut a melon

D-E:

Death Breath, Deflate, Doing the one-cheek sneak, Doorknob, Drifter, Drop one, Droppin' stink bombs, Duck call, Dial down under, Dutch Oven, Earth shaker, Empty the tank, Exhume the dinner corpse, Evict the egg salad.

F- G:

Fanny beep, Fanny clap, Fanny frog, Fart, Fecal fume, Fire a stink torpedo, Fire the retro rockets, Firing Scud Missiles, Fizzler, Flame thrower, Flamer, Flapper, Fire in the hole, Fizzler, Flatus, Floater, Float an air biscuit, Fluffy, Fowl howl, Fog slicer, Free jaccuzi, Free speech, Frump, Funky rollers, Gas, Gas attack, Glas blaster, Gassy grin, Get out and walk Donald, Great brown cloud, Grundle rumble, Grunt, Gurgler, Grumble down under.

H-K:

Hailing Emperor Crush, He who smelt it dealt it, Heinie hiccup, Hisser, Hole flapper, Honker, Horton hears a poo, Hot wind, Hottie, Human hydrogen bomb, Ignition, Insane in the methane, Jet propulsion, Jockey burner, Jumping guts, Just calling your name, K-fart, Kaboom, Kill the canary .

L-O:

Lay a wind loaf, Lay an egg, Let off, Let one rip, Let one go, Letting loose the thunder, Leave a gas trap, Let Polly out of jail, Let fluffy off the chain, Love puff, Man salute, Moon duck, Mouse on a motorcycle, Move the Nasty cough, Muff puff, O-ring oboe, One-man salute, One gun salute, Orchestra practice, Opening the basement window, Opening the air valve

P-R:

Painting the elevator, Panty strainer, Party in your pants, Panty burp, Pass gas, Pass wind, Peter, Pewie, Pip, Poof, Poop gopher, Poop gas, Pootsa, Pop tart Pop off, Popper, Power puff, Puff the magic dragon, Puffer, Putt-putt, Pump, Pumping, Quacker, Quaker, Raspberry, Rectal turbulence, Rim shot, Rip, Rip a juicy one, Ripper, Roar from the rear, Rump Rattler, Rump ripper, Rump ringer, Rump roar, Rumba down under.

S:

Salute your shorts, Shooting the canon, SBD (Silent but deadly), SBV (Silent but violent), SBS (Silent but scentless), Silly cyanide, Singe the carpet, Singing the anal anthem, Slider, Snart, Sphincter siren, Sphincter song Squeak one out, Sphincter whistle, Spit a brick, Spitter,

Split the seam, Squeaker, Stale wind, Stank rocket, Steam-press your Calvins, Steamer, Step on a duck, Step on a frog, Stink Burger, Stink it up, Stink press, Stinker, Stinky, Strangle the air pipe, Strangle the stank monkey, Stress release, Subterranean snarl.

T:

Tail wind, Taint tickle, Trouser trumpet, Tear ass, Testing in the Levi wind tunnel, The dog did it, The gluteal tuba, The sound and the fury, The stink's gone into the fabric, The third state of matter, The toothless one speaks, Thunder from down under, Thunder in the basement, Thurp, Toilet tune, Toot your own horn, Tootsie,

Trelblow, Triple flutter blast, Trouser cough, Trouser tremors, Turn on the A/C in your large intestine, Trunk bunk, Turtle burp, Tushy tickler

U-Z:

Uncorked symphony, Under burp, Under thunder, Wallop, Whiff, Whoopee, Whopper, Wrong way burp, Venting one, Zinger

Fart Onomatopoeia

Onomatopoeic words are words that sound like what they mean, so in making up onomatopoeic words for farts one might try to imagine how one would spell a fart sound phonetically.

For those that like to get creative with sound alike words, farts offer a whole world of opportunity to make up new words that reflect the wonderful range of sounds one can make when answering the call of the wild burrito.

The following selection is just the tip of the iceburg; see how many more

you can think of: Brrrt, Brarah, TRHPPTPHTPHPHHPH, Phhhhhhrt, PrPrPrPrPrPrPrPPPPPPPPP, Pfffft, Prrtrtrtrgurtrufrnasutututut, Phrrrt, PFFFT!, PHHhhhha..., SPLPLPLLLP, WHoooooofff, Poooot, Prrrvtrrrrvt, Scraeft, Prpppppwwarrrrppppp, Plplplplplplplplplplooooooooooooooaaa...,
RRRRRRRPPPPP, Fuuuuuuurrrrrrrt, Flhhhppbbbb, Vrrrrrrrrrnnnnnnnttttttt, plplplplplpbpbpbpbpbpbpbp, Pbpbpbpbp, Frrp frrp frrrrrrp rampoooooooooo ag,
Ppopopopopopoptttttttttttttttttttttttttttttt,

99

A Farty Farewell

Sadly we have reached the end of this farting odyessy. It's time to say "smell you later" and move on to other things.

If you take nothing else from your time exploring the magical world of gastric erruptions, remember this one simple fact:

You fart to live, you stop farting and you die!

So next time someone drops a foul stench in an elevator just smile, lift your nose high and take a deep whiff; after all their fart is a just celebration of this precious life that we all share.

Fart and be happy my friends...

Until next time
James Carlisle

Made in the USA
Monee, IL
08 March 2023

29465764R00057